A Bibliographical Guide to New Testament Research

Edited by R.T.France

JSOT Press

First edition by Tyndale Fellowship for Biblical Research 1968
Second edition by Tyndale Fellowship for Biblical Research 1974
Third edition by JSOT Press 1979
Reprint edition by JSOT Press 1983

ISBN O 905774 19 1

Published by
JSOT Press
Department of Biblical Studies
The University of Sheffield
Sheffield S1O 2TN
England

Printed in Great Britain by
Dotesios (Printers) Ltd.
Bradford-on-Avon, Wiltshire
1983

PREFACE

This is a revised version of a guide first
issued in duplicated form by the Tyndale Fellowship
for Biblical Research in 1968, and reprinted in the
journal Themelios vols. 5.4/6.1 (1969) pp. 11-31.
It was produced in response to the difficulty
experienced by New Testament research students in
finding information on specialised subjects related
to their field of study. Such information is
readily available in a good library, but students in
the early stages of research are often unaware of
where it is to be found. The continued demand for
the booklet led to a revised edition in 1974, and a
further revision has now been made to bring the
information up to date in August 1979. The original
contributors have been responsible for the revision,
though with the assistance of many who have used the
previous editions and have pointed out errors and
omissions.

It must be emphasised that this is not intended
at any point to be a complete bibliography of the
subject under consideration, but simply a guide to
sources of information. The subjects covered are
mainly concerned with background and reference; no
attempt has been made to provide bibliographies of
the more central areas of NT criticism, exegesis,
and theology, or of commentaries and other works on
individual books. (For commentaries, see New
Testament Commentary Survey by A.C. Thiselton,
revised by D.A. Carson, available from Theological
Students' Fellowship, 38 De Montfort Street,
Leicester.) On the less familiar subjects to which
NT students find themselves needing to refer (Qumran,
Rabbinics, etc.) we have indulged in rather more
detailed advice and information. Thus the differing
length of the sections is no indication of the
centrality of the subjects they treat, but rather of
their complexity or unfamiliarity to the average
student of the NT.

The Guide has been produced primarily with a
view to the British scene. English translations of
foreign works are listed, where they exist, and the

editions cited are British rather than American.
Section 1 applies only to British libraries.

The contributors are as follows:

R.T. France, Warden, Tyndale House, Cambridge
(editor).
A.R. Millard, Rankin Senior Lecturer in
Hebrew and Ancient Semitic Languages,
University of Liverpool.
G.N. Stanton, Professor of New Testament
Studies, University of London, King's
College.

CONTENTS

1. LIBRARY FACILITIES

The Copyright Regulations provide for one copy of every book published in Great Britain to be deposited in each of the National Libraries (British Library, Edinburgh, Aberystwyth, Dublin), and in the Bodleian Library, Oxford, and the Cambridge University Library. A list is published each week of books received at the Copyright Office of the British Library, under the title, The British National Bibliography, with monthly and annual indices. The British Library has made available copies of its Catalogue of Printed Books (263 vols. + 50 supp., 1968; 26 further supp. 1971-2), which can be consulted in the larger libraries. The Copyright Libraries do not lend out books except in special circumstances (or to graduates of the appropriate universities), but the National Central Library maintains a Union Catalogue, from which books can be located and borrowed. This is not open to public use, but operated by request through the Public Library system or through Inter-Library Loans. Although it is not always a speedy service, much effort is expended to obtain books and theses requested, sometimes drawing on continental sources. Periodicals may also be borrowed through this system, but it is quicker to make a check in the British Union Catalogue of Periodicals beforehand: this lists each periodical available in the co-operating libraries, with the names of the libraries holding it, and whether it may be taken from the library. Most University Libraries co-operate in the Inter-Library Loans system, by which books and unpublished theses may be borrowed from other University Libraries.

The British Library in London will issue a Reader's Ticket to an applicant who produces a supporting letter from, e.g., his tutor. In the Reading Room the catalogues and major reference works are to be found; all other books in the library will be fetched for readers, though the system can be slow.

In addition to the major libraries, considerable holdings in the NT field can be found at the following specialist libraries:

Sion College, London E.C.4
Dr. Williams' Library, 14 Gordon Square,
    London WC1H OAG (postal service;
    catalogues published to 1970)
St. Deiniol's Library, Hawarden, Cheshire
The Tyndale Library, 36 Selwyn Gardens,
    Cambridge CB3 9BA

Various diocesan libraries are useful, mainly for
older material, and some theological faculty or college libraries keep a good coverage of recent publications.

British library tradition arranges books by
author, within a subject classification, and catalogues are primarily author Catalogues. The British
Library issues a Subject Index of Modern Books every
five years, and other libraries maintain their own
Subject Catalogues. The Tyndale Library has a comprehensive subject index of articles in periodicals
and collected essays in areas relating to theology.

2. BIBLIOGRAPHICAL AIDS

(In this and the following section, the languages
used in periodicals are indicated as follows: E,
English; F, French; G, German; H, Hebrew; I, Italian;
L, Latin; Sp, Spanish; Sw, Swedish. Where no such
indication is given, the language is normally
English.)

The research student will constantly note references which are likely to aid his study, and it eases
the task if a consistent scheme is followed from the
beginning. Making references as complete as possible
from the start will avoid much time-consuming labour
in the later stages (i.e., publisher, series (if
any), place of publication, edition, and date);
unnecessary information can easily be omitted in
final writing (bibliographical conventions vary from
country to country, and even from university to university), but if your reference is insufficient, you

page 7

may have to go back to complete it. For this and
similar points, see B.M. Metzger, <u>A Guide to the
Preparation of a Thesis</u> (Princeton, 1961), bearing
in mind that it is geared to American practice.

When faced with a new field of study, the student is often at a loss to know where to seek published material. The first step should be examina-
tion of the basic text, then study of articles in
the standard reference works (see below sec. 10)
and pursuit of writings mentioned in their bibliographies. Thereafter, recourse may be made to the
following periodicals:-.

This is the one ↓ only journals

<u>New Testament Abstracts</u>, Weston College, Mass.,
thrice yearly since 1957; brief summaries of recent
books and articles, arranged by subject, with
Scripture, author, and journal indices.

<u>Elenchus Bibliographicus Biblicus</u> (L), Pontifical
Biblical Institute, Rome. Until 1968 contained in
<u>Biblica</u> (see sec. 3); now published separately each
year. The most comprehensive listing of books,
articles, Hebrew and Greek words discussed, and book
reviews (followed over years subsequent to the
publication of the books concerned), arranged by
subject, with full index; list of abbreviations at
beginning, table of contents at end. *This has books + journals
+ dissertations.*

<u>Religion Index One: Periodicals</u> (formerly <u>Index
to Religious Periodical Literature</u>), American
Theological Literary Association; published since
1955, and covering literature since 1949. Lists
articles and book reviews. Now appears twice
yearly, and in a cumulative volume every two years.

<u>Religious and Theological Abstracts</u>, Myerstown,
Pa., USA, quarterly since 1958, abstracts periodical
articles, with subject, author, and Scripture
indices.

<u>Religious Studies Review</u> (Council on the Study of
Religion, USA). Quarterly since 1975.

<u>Internationale Zeitschriftenschau für</u>

Bibelwissenschaft und Grenzgebiete (EFG), Patmos
Verlag, Düsseldorf; annual since 1952; similar to
NT Abstracts, but covering a wider subject-area;
author index.

Other periodicals contain regular bibliographical features: note particularly Zeitschrift für die
neutestamentliche Wissenschaft, Theologische
Zeitschrift, and Evangelische Theologie.

Naturally there is an interval between the
publication of a work and its appearance in these
lists. To keep right up to date watch publishers'
advertisements in periodicals. New British publications are listed quickly in the British National
Bibliography (see sec. 1), classified by the Dewey
Decimal System. Forthcoming American books are
noted in Christianity Today each February.

All of the above are, of course, piecemeal, and
subjects need to be followed through each year. The
following non-recurrent bibliographies will save time
in tracing work up to their date of publication:

St. John's University Library Index to Biblical
Journals (St. John's University Press, Collegeville,
Minnesota, 1971), a computer-generated cumulative
index to some of the major journals, covering the
last fifty years or so.

P.-E. Langevin, Bibliographie Biblique 1930-1970
(Université Laval, Quebec, 1972), a very full listing
of articles in Catholic journals and other Catholic
publications. A second volume, extending to non-
Catholic publications, is promised.

B.M. Metzger, Index of Articles on the NT and Early
Church published in Festschriften (Society of
Biblical Literature, Philadelphia, 1951) covering
Festschriften published up to early 1950; a supple-
ment (1955) brings the coverage up to the end of 1950.

Many dissertations, esp. American, are indexed
annually in Dissertation Abstracts International
(Xerox University Microfilms, Ann Arbor). A wider

field was included in <u>Comprehensive Dissertation
Index</u> (ibid, 1973), a 37-volume cumulative listing
of dissertations in the period 1861-1972 (vol. 32
covers Philosophy and Religion); annual supplements
since 1974. For British theses since 1950 see the
annual <u>Index to Theses</u> published by Aslib; for those
prior to 1950 see R.R. Bilboul (ed.), <u>Index to Theses
of Great Britain and Ireland 1716-1950</u> (American
Bibliographical Center, Santa Barbara, CA, 1975)-
vol. 1 covers humanities. Most British theses since
about 1970 may be loaned on microfilm from the
British Library Lending Division.

Some subjects have their own specialised bibliographies, e.g.:

B.M. Metzger, <u>Index to Periodical Literature on the
Apostle Paul</u> (E.J. Brill, Leiden, 1960).

B.M. Metzger, <u>Index to Periodical Literature on
Christ and the Gospels</u> (E.J. Brill, Leiden, 1966). *reference section at Bethel*

A.J. Mattill, Jr. & M.B. Mattill, <u>A Classified
Bibliography of Literature on the Acts of the
Apostles</u> (E.J. Brill, Leiden, 1966).

E. Malatesta, <u>St. John's Gospel 1920-1965</u> (Biblical
Institute Press, Rome, 1967).

For other such bibliographies see the very
useful <u>Bibliography of NT Bibliographies</u>, by J.C.
Hurd, Jr. (Seabury Press, New York, 1966); very
comprehensive, covering bibliographical sources for
individual books and sections of the NT, special
subjects, and major NT scholars.

Selective bibliographies for NT studies in
general include the following:

F.W. Danker, <u>Multipurpose Tools for Bible Study</u>
(Concordia, St. Louis, 1966), with essays on <u>how to</u>
<u>use</u> the major tools of biblical exegesis.

D.M. Scholer, A Basic Bibliographic Guide for NT
Exegesis (Eerdmans, Grand Rapids, 1973); similar in

get this one

O.T. Commentary Survey by I.V.P.

scope to the present Guide.

W.G. Kümmel, <u>Introduction to the NT</u> (ET, SCM, London, rev. ed. 1975) pp. 23-27, a list of 'The Most Important tools for the Study of the NT'.

Further bibliographies on specific subjects treated in this Guide are mentioned below in sec. 5 (Textual Criticism), sec. 17 (Semitic Languages), sec. 18 (Targums), sec. 21 (Apocrypha and Pseudepigrapha), sec. 22 (Qumran), sec. 23 (Philo & Josephus), sec. 24 (Judaism), and sec. 25 (Nag Hammadi).

3. PERIODICALS

This list is not, of course, exhaustive, but aims to draw attention to those periodicals which are likely to provide material of service to the NT scholar, and to mention any special characteristics.

The following classification has been attempted:

      1. Vital for NT study.
      2. Worth watching for relevant articles.
      3. Dealing with specialised areas of relevance to the NT.
      4. Valuable for book reviews.

(For language classification, see beginning of sec. 2)

<u>Biblica</u> (2, EFGILSp) Catholic; some useful articles; mainly valuable for bibliography (see sec. 2, 5).
<u>Biblical Archaeologist</u> (2) Includes surveys of recent discoveries, and translations of important articles in other languages.
<u>Biblical Research</u> (2) Chicago Society of Biblical Research. Occasional important articles; some light-weight.
<u>Biblical Theology Bulletin</u> (2) Includes useful

survey articles particularly by Catholic
scholars.
Biblische Zeitschrift (2, EFG) A useful guide to the
approach of Catholic scholars.
Bulletin of the American Schools of Oriental Research
(3) Archaeological studies in the Near East.
Bulletin of the John Rylands Library (2) Not very
many biblical articles, but sometimes important.
Catholic Biblical Quarterly (1, 4) The voice of
American Catholic scholarship. One of the best
for reviews.
Churchman (4) Evangelical Anglican; articles seldom
of importance for NT studies, but some excellent
reviews.
The Evangelical Quarterly (2, 4) The academic level
or articles and reviews varies considerably.
Evangelische Theologie (2, G) Mainly systematic
theology. Quarterly Beiheft surveys recent
books - one a year on NT.
Expository Times (2, 4) Much that is light-weight, or
irrelevant to NT study, but some valuable
articles and surveys of scholarship.
Harvard Theological Review (2) Biblical articles tend
to be specialised; some very useful philological
notes.
Interpretation (2, 4) Union Theological Seminary,
Virginia. Carries some major papers.
Israel Exploration Journal (3, EF) Archaeological
work in Israel.
Jewish Quarterly Review (3) American.
Journal of Biblical Literature (1, 4) The leading
American periodical in the NT field.
Journal of the Evangelical Theological Society (2)
American evangelical scholarship.
Journal of Jewish Studies (3).
Journal of Religion (2) American, covering a wide
field; occasional useful biblical articles.
Journal for the Study of Judaism in the Persian,
Hellenistic and Roman Period (3, 4, EFG) Each
issue includes a review of relevant articles.
Journal for the Study of the New Testament (1) Began
1978, to provide for rapid publication of
articles for NT specialists. Already important.
Journal of Theological Studies (1, 4) Articles few
and detailed; many important 'Short Notes';

vast array of book reviews.

New Testament Studies (1, EFG) Needs no praise!

Novum Testamentum (1, 4, EFG) Second only to NTS.

Palestine Exploration Quarterly (3) For archaeology
    and topography.

Religious Studies (2, 4) Rare, but valuable, articles
    of relevance to NT.

Review and Expositor (2) Southern Baptist. Fall
    issue each year focuses on one biblical book.

Revue Biblique (1, 4, F) Includes surveys of current
    archaeological exploration, besides much excel-
    lent Catholic biblical scholarship.

Revue de Qumran (3, EFG) See sec. 22.

Scottish Journal of Theology (2, 4) Some important
    biblical studies, esp. (but by no means always)
    from a Barthian angle.

Semeia (2) Exploratory papers by American biblical
    scholars. Irregular publication.

Studia Theologica (2, EFG) 'Scandinavian Journal of
    Theology'; but not all Scandinavian. Some
    important articles, esp. in German.

Svensk Exegetisk Årsbok (2, SwEG) Some of the best
    of Scandinavian biblical study.

Textus (3, EFH) Deals with individual Hebrew texts
    (including initial publication) and Rabbinic
    study.

Themelios (formerly TSF Bulletin) (2, 4) Includes
    occasional valuable extended reviews and
    surveys of recent scholarship.

Theological Studies (2) Catholic. Some important
    articles on Oxyrhynchus, Gospel of Thomas, etc.

Theologische Literaturzeitung (4, G) Book reviews
    cover all areas of theological study.

Theologische Rundschau (2, G) Includes very valuable
    surveys of scholarship in particular areas,
    and reviews of major books.

Theologische Zeitschrift (2, 4, EFG) From Basel
    Theological Faculty.

Theology (2, 4) Articles brief, but sometimes
    valuable.

Tyndale Bulletin (2) Conservative biblical studies.
    Contains some of the Tyndale Lectures.

Vetus Testamentum (2, EFG) Virtually OT equivalent
    of Novum Testamentum.

Vigiliae Christianae (3, EFGI) Covers early Church
    history, including Gnostic material.

<u>Vox Evangelica</u> (2) London Bible College. Many
    biblical articles.
\<u>Westminster Theological Journal</u> (2) Conservative
    American. *book reviews* . . .
<u>Zeitschrift für die alttestamentliche Wissenschaft</u>
    (2, EFG) OT equivalent of following; each
    article followed by summary in the other two
    languages. Its <u>Zeitschriftenschau</u> is inval-
    uable.
<u>Zeitschrift für die neutestamentlische Wissenschaft</u>
    (1, EFG) Its <u>Zeitschriftenschau</u> is a valuable
    feature (see sec. 2).
<u>Zeitschrift für Theologie und Kirche</u> (2, G) Some now
    famous articles of the Bultmann school first
    appeared here; useful for NT theology and
    hermeneutics. Some of the more important
    articles have been translated into English
    in <u>Journal for Theology and the Church</u>, begun
    1965.

4. <u>TEXTS OF THE NEW TESTAMENT</u>

The standard text used by most NT scholars is
E. Nestle - K. Aland (ed.) <u>Novum Testamentum Graece</u>
(Württembergische Bibelanstalt, Stuttgart) 25th ed.,
1963; a substantially revised 26th ed. is promised
for September 1979.

<u>The Greek New Testament</u>, ed. K. Aland, M. Black,
C.M. Martini, B.M. Metzger, A. Wikgren (United Bible
Societies, 3rd ed. 1975) contains the same text as
the forthcoming 26th edition of Nestle-Aland. Its
critical apparatus cites fewer variants, but with
much fuller evidence for those cited.

K. Aland has a useful article on 'The Greek NT:
its Present and Future Editions', <u>JBL</u> 87 (1968) 179-
186. Note also the following article in <u>JBL</u> 87.

5. TEXTUAL CRITICISM

This is a vast and specialised field, in which the beginner should tread warily. B.M. Metzger, The Text of the NT: its Transmission, Corruption and Restoration[2] (Clarendon Press, Oxford, 1968) will provide all the basic information for most students, and includes good bibliographical data for those following up some point in detail. Less comprehensive, but good for whetting the beginner's appetite, is J. Finegan, Encountering NT Manuscripts (SPCK, London, 1975).

For a very brief introduction to the principles of 'Rational Criticism' see J.K. Elliott, Theology 75 (1972) 338-343. More fully, J.N. Birdsall in The Cambridge History of the Bible, Vol. I, ed. P.R. Ackroyd & C.F. Evans (Cambridge UP, 1970), pp. 308-377.

A continuing bibliography of NT textual criticism by J. Duplacy is published in Biblica, beginning vol. 49 (1968) 515-551; there is one bibliography for every two years, published in two halves, one each year. Earlier bibliographies by Duplacy were published in Recherches de Science Religieuse 1962-3 and 1965-6. NB also B.M. Metzger, An Annotated Bibliography of the Textual Criticism of the NT, 1914-1939 (Munksgaard, Copenhagen, 1955).

For the versions, see the definitive treatment by B.M. Metzger, The Early Versions of the NT: their Origin, Transmission and Limitations (Clarendon Press, Oxford, 1977).

For specific textual points, see a good critical commentary, and also B.M. Metzger, A Textual Commentary on the Greek NT (United Bible Societies, 1971) - a companion volume to the UBS Greek NT (see sec. 4). The Introduction gives a convenient summary of guiding principles, and a listing of text-families.

6. SYNOPSES ~ *Aland*

K. Aland (ed.), <u>Synopsis Quattuor Evangeliorum</u>
(Württembergische Bibelanstalt, Stuttgart, 10th ed.
1978) can be expected to remain the standard synopsis
for many decades. Established scholars will continue
to use well-marked copies of Huck's Synopsis, but
Aland offers many advantages over Huck. Particularly useful are the following: inclusion of the
Fourth Gospel; inclusion of the most important
parallels from the NT Apocrypha and the Church
Fathers; appendices with translations of the Gospel
of Thomas; Greek and Latin texts of all the most
important <u>Testimonia Patrum Veterum</u> (Papias, etc.);
good cross-references and textual variants. The
Greek-English edition, <u>Synopsis of the Four Gospels</u>[3]
(ibid, 1979) omits the material from apocryphal
gospels and church fathers, the Gospel of Thomas,
and the <u>Testimonia Patrum Veterum</u>. The latest
editions of both versions have been updated to
correspond to the 26th edition of Nestle-Aland.

The multi-coloured method of W.R. Farmer,
<u>Synopticon</u> (Cambridge UP, 1969) may sometimes be
helpful in showing at a glance the extent of verbal
agreement in a passage, but it is generally safer
and more convenient to have synoptic texts printed
side by side as in a traditional synopsis.

Another 'visual aid' is R.J. Swanson, <u>The
Horizontal Line Synopsis of the Gospels</u> (Western
North Carolina Press, 1975), which prints the
parallels under one another, underlining areas of
agreement. In English; Greek edition promised.

Other older synopses may still be of some use,
particularly B. de Solages', <u>A Greek Synopsis of the
Gospels</u> (E.J. Brill, Leiden, 1959).

A synopsis with a difference is R. Morgenthaler,
<u>Statistische Synopse</u> (Gotthelf-Verlag, Zürich, 1971).
After discussing the approaches of selected earlier
synopses, without actually printing the text, it sets
out statistically the degree of verbal agreement, and
the variations in the orders of the words, sentences

and sections, and goes on to draw conclusions for the
Synoptic Problem. A forbidding book, but full of
valuable information for the specialist on the
Synoptic Problem.

7. NEW TESTAMENT CONCORDANCES

The definitive concordance is now K. Aland et al
(ed.), Vollständige Konkordanz zum griechischen NT
(De Gruyter, Berlin) vol. I. Began to appear in
1975, and should be complete by about 1982. (A stop-
gap Computer-Konkordanz covering z-ō has been issued
for the use of those who cannot wait!) Gives longer
lemmata than most concordances, and even kai appears
in full. Up-to-date textual data, based on the 26th
ed. of Nestle-Aland. A vol. II (1978) gives very
full statistical data on distribution of vocabulary,
frequency of word-forms, hapax legomena, &c.

The Concordance to the Greek NT of W.F. Moulton
and A.S. Geden (T. & T. Clark, Edinburgh, 4th ed.
1963) is thus superseded. Those who continue to use
it (and few will be able to buy Aland!) must remember that it is based on the 1881 Westcott & Hort
text and the 1875 ed. of Tischendorf's text. (The
fifth ed., 1977, is identical apart from the correc-
tion of a few misprints and the printing out in full
of the entries for some common prepositions, etc.
previously listed by chapter and verse only.)

Still useful for Synoptic criticism are Sir
John Hawkins' lists of words and phrases in Horae
Synopticae: Contributions to the Study of the
Synoptic Problem (2nd ed. 1909). Again the WH
text is used.

L. Gaston, Horae Synopticae Electronicae: Word
Statistics of the Synoptic Gospels (Society of
Biblical Literature, 1973) is an attempt to do the
same job more precisely with the aid of a computer,
taking into account the postulates of form-
criticism, and more recent views on sources.

The references in Bauer-Arndt-Gingrich's
Lexicon (sec. 8) can also double as a concordance,
but there is not always a full listing of occurrences.

Particularly useful for any type of
Vokabelstatistik work is R. Morgenthaler, Statistik
des neutestamentlichen Wortschatzes (Gotthelf-
Verlag, Zürich, 1958). It contains a lengthy introduction, and detailed tables giving the occurrences
of a word in the different NT books, which eliminate
a lot of tedious word-counting!

X. Jacques, List of NT Words Sharing Common
Elements: Supplement to Concordance or Dictionary
(Biblical Institute Press, Rome, 1969) groups
together words from the same root, which in a
dictionary or concordance are necessarily separated
by alphabetic arrangement. A great help.

8. GREEK LEXICA

Bauer-Arndt-Gingrich's A Greek-English Lexicon
of the NT and other Early Christian Literature[2]
(Chicago UP, 1979) needs no introduction. (Often
abbreviated AG in English works.) Many entries
include good bibliographies, on problem verses as
well as on a word in general. The English translation is a revised version of the 5th German ed.
(1958). Users of the first edition of AG (1957)
should be aware that it was based on the 4th German
edition; the 1979 edition incorporates extensive
revisions both by Bauer and by his translators.

Liddell and Scott's A Greek-English Lexicon
(Clarendon Press, Oxford; new (9th) ed. 1940;
supplement 1968) is the standard work for classical
Greek, and is valuable for Hellenistic Greek in
general, including the LXX, but it should not be
used for the NT and Church Fathers.

More specialised, but old, is E.A. Sophocles,

Greek Lexicon of the Roman and Byzantine Periods
(146 BC - AD 1100) (rev. ed. 1887; reprinted Olms,
Hildesheim, 1975).

See below sec. 25 for Lampe's Patristic Greek
Lexicon.

9. GREEK GRAMMARS

The standard work is A Greek Grammar of the NT
and other Early Christian Literature, by F. Blass,
ed. A. Debrunner; ed. and translated by R.W. Funk
(Cambridge UP, 1961) - generally referred to as
Blass-Debrunner (Bl-D). Much fuller, and used widely
esp. in America, is A.T. Robertson, A Grammar of the
Greek NT in the Light of Historical Research (1914,
now reprinted by Broadman, Nashville TN).

Also valuable are: Grammar of NT Greek, J.H.
Moulton et al (T. & T. Clark, Edinburgh): vol. 1,
3rd ed. 1908; vol. 2 (W.F. Howard) 1929; vol. 3
(N. Turner) 1963; vol. 4 (N. Turner) 1976; An Idiom-
Book of NT Greek, C.F.D. Moule (Cambridge UP, 1959)
- classicists, who should beware of reading classical
Greek grammar and syntax into the NT, would find
Moule's book a valuable corrective.

All these have good indices, with references to
NT passages cited and discussed - very useful for
exegesis of particular passages. *M. Zerwick - grammar BiblioGreek.*

10. DICTIONARIES AND ENCYCLOPAEDIAS

The NT research worker should know the
strengths and weaknesses of the standard reference
works; much time can be saved if one knows where
succinct articles and bibliographical references on
particular subjects can be found. The following are
listed alphabetically:-

Biblisch-historisches Handwörterbuch: Landeskunde, Geschichte, Religion, Kultur, Literatur, ed. B. Reicke & L. Rost (Vandenhoeck & Ruprecht, Göttingen, 1962-1966) 3 vols. Index volume in preparation. Useful for background materials, and a little more wide-ranging on this than NBD, but often thin.

→International Standard Bible Encyclopaedia *in Revised ed.* (Eerdmans, Grand Rapids, 1929) 5 vols. The standard large-scale American conservative work. A new, completely revised, ed. to be published soon - long expected! (Abbrev. ISBE)

→Interpreter's Dictionary of the Bible (Abingdon Press, New York, 1962) 4 vols; supplementary vol. 1976. Justly the most widely-used large-scale Bible dictionary. Particularly useful for bibliographies. (Abbrev. IDB)

Lexikon zur Bibel, ed. F. Rienecker (Brockhaus Verlag, Wuppertal, 1960) 1 vol. Well-produced German equivalent of NBD.

New Bible Dictionary, ed. J.D. Douglas (IVF, London, 1962) 1 vol. Completely revised ed., ed. N. Hillyer, expected 1980. Value out of proportion to its size. Good bibliographies, slanted towards conservative literature, but not exclusively so. (Abbrev. NBD)

New International Dictionary of NT Theology, ed. C. Brown (Paternoster, Exeter, 1975-8) 3 vols. English ed. of Theologisches Begriffslexikon below, but revised and considerably expanded by English-speaking scholars, and rearranged under English alphabetical order. Very full bibliographies. A most valuable resource. (Abbrev. NIDNTT)

Oxford Dictionary of the Christian Church, ed. F.L. Cross (2nd ed., Oxford UP, 1974) 1 vol. A mine of information on church history, though not always accurate. Good basic bibliographies.

Peake's Commentary on the Bible, ed. M. Black & H.H. Rowley (Nelson, London, 1962) has useful general articles. (A complete rewriting of the 1920 ed.)

Reallexikon für Antike und Christentum: Sachwörterbuch zur Auseinandersetzung des Christentums mit der antiken Welt, ed. T. Klauser (Hiersemann, Stuttgart, 1950 ff), 10 vols. so far. Exactly what the title says; invaluable, and on a

massive scale - the last two vols. have been in the
Ge- area! (Abbrev. RAC)
   Die Religion in Geschichte und Gegenwart (Mohr,
Tübingen, 3rd ed., 1957-1965) 7 vols. A mine of
information, including many articles on NT subjects
(e.g. H. Conzelmann's much cited Jesus Christus),
and excellent bibliographies of German works.
(Abbrev. RGG)
   Supplément au Dictionnaire de la Bible, originally
ed. L. Pirot, now ed. H. Cazelles & A. Feuillet
(Letouzey & Ané, Paris, 1928 ff) 9 vols. to date.
Early fascicles of vol. 10 have reached into R.
Earlier vols. now well out of date, but more recent
vols. provide excellent French Catholic scholarship,
with full coverage of recent literature on each
subject.
   Theologisches Begriffslexikon zum NT, ed. L.
Coenen, E. Beyreuther, H. Bietenhard (Brockhaus,
Wuppertal, 1965-1971) 3 vols. Similar to Kittel,
though on a much smaller scale. Conservative (by
German standards). Articles follow the alphabetical
order of the German, not Greek, words. For English
edition, see NIDNTT, above.
   Theologisches Wörterbuch zum NT, ed. G. Kittel
(later G. Friedrich) (Kohlhammer Verlag, Stuttgart,
1933 ff) (Abbrev. TWNT). English trans. ed. G.W.
Bromiley (Eerdmans, Grand Rapids, 1964 ff) (Abbrev.
TDNT). 9 vols. plus index vol. Needs no praise.
But a Kittel article should not be taken as the last
word on a given subject; some articles in the
earlier vols. are now well out of date; the first
chapter of D. Hill, Greek Words and Hebrew Meanings
(Cambridge UP, 1967) has a good discussion of James
Barr's now well known criticisms of the basic
approach of Kittel.
   Zondervan Pictorial Encyclopedia of the Bible
(Zondervan, Grand Rapids, 1975) 5 vols. American,
very conservative, generally up-to-date. (Abbrev.
ZPEB).

   Several older works contain standard basic
studies, notably Hastings' Dictionary of the Bible
(T. & T. Clark, Edinburgh, 1900) 5 vols. (Abbrev.
HDB)

Other more specialised reference works are
listed below: see esp. sec. 24.1 for <u>Encyclopaedia
Judaica</u>, now one of the most up-to-date reference
works for all aspects of Jewish history, culture,
etc.

11. <u>NEW TESTAMENT INTRODUCTION</u>

The literature here is voluminous. The following will help in orientation on a particular subject,
and will provide bibliographical information:-

W.G. Kümmel, <u>Introduction to the NT</u> (ET, SCM,
London, rev. ed., 1975). A tremendous amount of
highly compressed information, with bibliographies
covering French and English works as well as German.
Good sections on the <u>text</u> and <u>canon</u> of the NT. Pp.
29-34 list all significant NT introductions published
up to 1971. A useful extended review of the first
ed. by A.C. Thiselton appeared in <u>TSF Bulletin</u> nos.
49, 51 and 52 (1967-1968).
D. Guthrie, <u>NT Introduction</u> (Tyndale Press,
London, 1961-1965; one-vol. ed. 1970). The standard
conservative introduction, remarkable for its full
coverage of literature, and fairness to all views
discussed.
A. Wikenhauser, <u>NT Introduction</u>[2] (ET, Herder,
Dublin, 1958). A standard Catholic work, with
useful material on <u>text</u> and <u>canon</u>.
W. Marxsen, <u>Introduction to the NT</u>[3] (ET, Blackwell,
Oxford, 1968). Intentionally less detailed than the
above, in order to emphasise the 'theological
approach' dominant in current German NT study.

For the history of NT scholarship, see the
following:

S. Neill, <u>The Interpretation of the NT, 1861-1961</u>
(Oxford UP, 1964). Emphasis on British scholarship.
W.G. Kümmel, <u>The NT, The History of the Investiga-
tion of its Problem</u>s (ET, SCM, London, 1973).
Emphasis on German scholarship.

R.H. Fuller, The NT in Current Study (SCM, London, 1963). A useful brief introduction to the Bultmann school, 1941-1962.
The Cambridge History of the Bible (Cambridge UP, 1963-1970). The relevant sections of the 3 vols. give a convenient survey of the history of biblical study.

Some of the problems raised by the various critical methods, and their effect on NT interpretation are discussed in the following:-

G.E. Ladd, The NT and Criticism (Hodder, London, 1970) by a leading American conservative scholar.
O. Kaiser & W.G. Kümmel, Exegetical Method (ET, Seabury Press, New York, 1967).
I.H. Marshall (ed.), New Testament Interpretation (Paternoster, Exeter, 1977) includes discussion of critical methods by members of the Tyndale Fellowship.

12. NEW TESTAMENT HISTORY

F.F. Bruce, NT History (Nelson/Oliphants, London, 1969) is the most generally useful brief account of NT history as a whole. Its value lies particularly in the full coverage of the wider background to NT history.
F.V. Filson, A NT History (SCM, London, 1965) is also useful. (NB the list on pp. 429-432 of British editions of American books cited in the notes.)
L. Goppelt, Apostolic and Post-Apostolic Times (ET, A. & C. Black, London, 1970) is not so full on background, but excellent on the internal development of the church.

For the historical background to NT history see also:-

J. Leipoldt & W. Grundmann, Umwelt des Urchristentums; Vol. 1, Darstellung des NT

Zeitalters[2] (Evangelische Verlagsanstalt, Berlin,
1967). Vol. 2 of the same work (Texte zum NT
Zeitalter, 1967) gives a wide selection of source
material, arranged according to the contents of vol.
1. There is also a vol. 3 of pictures (1966).
    B. Reicke, The NT Era (ET, A. & C. Black, London,
1969). Briefer, but packed with information.
    C.K. Barrett, The NT Background: Selected
Documents (SPCK, London, 1956). Useful source
material on history, philosophy, religion, literature, etc.
    E. M. Smallwood, The Jews under Roman Rule: from
Pompey to Diocletian (E.J. Brill, Leiden, 1976) is
one of the fullest histories of the period.

    The first part of the massive project Compendia
Rerum Iudaicarum ad Novum Testamentum is a two-
volume symposium on The Jewish People in the First
Century, ed. S. Safrai and M. Stern (Van Gorcum,
Assen, 1974 and 1976) containing 24 studies of
aspects of Jewish history, culture and religion.
Good indices and survey of contents in vol. 2.

    See also the works listed in sec. 20 below, esp.
Schürer and Jeremias. Also relevant entries in the
reference works listed in sec. 10.

    NB also F.J. Foakes Jackson & K. Lake (ed.),
The Beginnings of Christianity: Part I, The Acts of
the Apostles (Macmillan, London, 1920-1935) 5 vols.
Vol. 1 contains useful material on the historical
background of the NT, and vols. 4 (commentary) and 5
(additional notes) should be consulted on subjects
directly related to Acts. (Vols. 4 & 5 reprinted by
Baker, Grand Rapids, 1966).

    For a very comprehensive and up-to-date
coverage of one special area see H. Hoehner, Herod
Antipas (Cambridge UP, 1972) - excellent bibliographies.

    For chronological matters, a useful guide to a
very complex subject is J. Finegan, Handbook of
Biblical Chronology: Principles of Time Reckoning
in the Ancient World and Problems of Chronology

in the Bible (Princeton UP, 1964). See also G. Ogg,
The Chronology of the Public Ministry of Jesus
(Cambridge UP, 1940) and The Chronology of the Life
of Paul (Epworth, London, 1968); also H.W. Hoehner,
Chronological Aspects of the Life of Christ
(Zondervan, Grand Rapids, 1977), which combines
controversial views with much valuable factual data.

13. TOPOGRAPHY

    The best of many Bible atlases for historical
purposes remains L.H. Grollenberg, Atlas of the Bible
(Nelson, London, 1956). The condensed form, A
Shorter Atlas of the Bible (Penguin, 1978) is also
very good value. Environmental factors are more
fully set out in D. Baly & A.D. Tushingham, Atlas
of the Biblical World (World Publishing Co., New
York, 1971).

    Historical geography of Palestine is given up-
to-date treatment by M. Avi-Yonah, The Holy Land from
the Persian to the Arab Conquests (Baker, Grand
Rapids, 1966), helpfully set out, with references.
The 25th ed. of G. Adam Smith, Historical Geography
of the Holy Land (Hodder & Stoughton, London, 1931;
repr. Fontana, 1966) remains standard, though dated.
See also, for topological and ecological data, D.
Baly, The Geography of the Bible² (Lutterworth,
London, 1974): also his Geographical Companion to the
Bible (Lutterworth, London, 1963).

    For the area of Paul's travels, see H. Metzger,
St. Paul's Journeys in the Greek Orient (SCM, London,
1955). The brief survey of knowledge in Metzger can
be supplemented from section III of The Biblical
Archaeologist Reader, Vol. 2, ed. E.F. Campbell &
D.N. Freedman (Anchor, New York, 1964), entitled
'Prominent Cities of the NT Period'. The works of
Sir William Ramsay are also still important.

14. NEW TESTAMENT ARCHAEOLOGY

Many (but not all) books on biblical archaeology
include discoveries relating to the NT, e.g. D.J.
Wiseman, Illustrations from Biblical Archaeology[3]
(Tyndale Press, London, 1966); J.A. Thompson, The
Bible and Archaeology (Paternoster, Exeter, re. ed.
1973), which is fuller than most on the NT period.
For a succinct survey see F.F. Bruce, 'Archaeological
Confirmation of the NT' in Revelation and the Bible,
ed. C.F.H. Henry (Tyndale Press, London, 1959) 319-
331.

An up-to-date reference work, set out alphabetically under sites, is M. Avi-Yonah (ed.) Encyclopaedia of Archaeological Excavations in the Holy
Land (Massada Press, Jerusalem and OUP, 1975 ff) 4
vols.

The most helpful introductory work is R.K.
Harrison, Teach Yourself Archaeology of the NT (EUP,
1964; reprinted as paperback (Archaeology of the NT)
by Hodder, London, 1967). Harrison covers the
ground adequately, and his many references provide a
useful guide to more detailed treatments of
individual subjects.

Fuller and more recent is J. Finegan, The
Archaeology of the NT (Princeton UP, 1969), dealing
mainly with the life of Jesus; i.e. almost exclusively Palestinian archaeology. See, however, the
review article by J.P. Kane in Religion 2 (1972) 57-
75 for some basic criticisms of Finegan's method,
and many valuable references.

15. PAPYROLOGY

The classic survey of results in this field is
A. Deissmann, Light from the Ancient East[4] (ET,
Hodder & Stoughton, London, 1927; repr. Baker, Grand
Rapids, 1965). The standard reference work is J.H.
Moulton & G. Milligan, The Vocabulary of the Greek

Testament, Illustrated from the Papyri (H & S, London, 1930) (Abbrev. MM). Examples are gathered in G. Milligan, Selections from the Greek Papyri (Cambridge UP, 1910).

It will be seen that these are old works; the field is wide open for workers. The techniques and categories of material are well treated by E.G. Turner, Greek Papyri, An Introduction (Clarendon Press, Oxford, 1968), with bibliographies of major reference works and collections of papyri, and illustrated in his Greek Manuscripts of the Ancient World (Clarendon Press, Oxford, 1971).

A collection of particular importance for the NT student is V.A. Tcherikover, A. Fuks, M. Stern (eds.), Corpus Papyrorum Judaicarum (Harvard UP, Cambridge, Mass., 1957-1964) 3 vols.

An important tool for the specialist (only!) is K. Aland (ed.), Repertorium der griechischen christlichen Papyri (de Gruyter, Berlin); vol. 1 (1976) covers biblical papyri.

16. CLASSICAL HEBREW

As the NT derives so much from the OT, it would be foolish to embark on NT research without at least enough knowledge to follow the Hebrew text, and use lexica, concordance, etc.

1. Old Testament Text

The standard critical edition by R. Kittel, P. Kahle, Biblia Hebraica[3] (Württembergische Bibelanstalt, Stuttgart, 1937 ff) has now been replaced by Biblia Hebraica Stuttgartensia (ibid, 1977), ed. K. Elliger, W. Rudolph. The textual notes at the foot of each page include many critical emendations (more in the 1937 edition than in the 1977) and are to be treated with caution. They are not a simple <u>apparatus criticus</u>. The British and Foreign Bible Society publishes N.H. Snaith's slightly different text, without annotation or distinction of poetic passages in prose works (<u>Hebrew Old Testament</u>, 1958).

2. Grammars

J. Weingreen, <u>A Practical Grammar of Classical Hebrew</u>[2] (Clarendon Press, Oxford, 1959). The most straight-forward for learning.

T.O. Lambdin, <u>Introduction to Biblical Hebrew</u> (Darton, Longman & Todd, London, 1973). More informative than Weingreen.

A.B. Davidson, <u>An Introductory Hebrew Grammar</u>[25], revised by J. Mauchline (T. & T. Clark, Edinburgh, 1962).

F.H.W. Gesenius, ed. E. Kautzsch, <u>Hebrew Grammar</u>, trans. & ed. A.E. Cowley (Clarendon Press, Oxford, reprint 1946 and frequently since). The standard large-scale reference work. (Abbrev. GK)

3. Dictionaries

F. Brown, S.R. Driver, & C.A. Briggs, <u>Hebrew and English Lexicon of the OT</u> (Clarendon Press, Oxford, 1906 ff; repr. 1952). (Abbrev. BDB)

L. Köhler & W. Baumgartner, <u>Hebräisches und aramäisches Lexicon zum AT</u> (E.J. Brill, Leiden, 1948-1953; supp. 1958; 3rd ed. 1967-   ). (Abbrev. KB) See J.A. Emerton's review of the 3rd ed., <u>VT</u> 25 (1975) 810-816.

W. L. Holladay, <u>A Concise Hebrew and Aramaic Lexicon of the OT</u> (E.J. Brill, Leiden, 1971). A shortened version of KB, very convenient for quick reference, and much more adequate than Fohrer's <u>Dictionary</u>.

4. Concordances

S. Mandelkern, <u>Veteris Testamenti Concordantiae</u> (Graz, 1937; repr. Schocken, Tel Aviv, 1969).

G. Lisowsky, <u>Konkordanz zum hebräisches AT</u>
(Württembergische Bibelanstalt, Stuttgart, 1958) –
more recent, less complete, but with pointed Hebrew.

17. <u>LATER HEBREW AND ARAMAIC</u>

For an excellent introduction to Mishnaic
Hebrew, drawing on recent work in Israel, see E.Y.
Kutscher in <u>Encyclopaedia Judaica</u> (on which see sec.
24 below), vol. 16, cols. 1590-1607. Kutscher gives
a valuable introduction to Aramaic, <u>ibid</u>., vol. 2,
cols. 263-287.

1. <u>Grammars</u>

M. Segal, <u>Mishnaic Hebrew Grammar</u>[2] (Clarendon
Press, Oxford, 1958).
W.B. Stevenson, <u>Grammar of Palestinian Jewish
Aramaic</u> (Clarendon Press, Oxford, 1962).
G. Dalman, <u>Grammatik des jüdisch-palästinischen
Aramäisch</u>[2] (1905; repr. Wissenschaftliche
Buchgesellschaft, Darmstadt, 1960).
F. Rosenthal, <u>A Grammar of Biblical Aramaic</u>
(Harrassowitz, Wiesbaden, 1961).

2. <u>Dictionaries</u>

Mishnaic and New Hebrew are not separated from
Aramaic in the lexica.

G. Dalman, <u>Aramäisch-neuhebräisches
Handwörterbuch</u>[2] (Kauffmann, Frankfurt, 1922).
M. Jastrow, <u>Dictionary of the Targumim, the Talmud
Babli and Yerushalmi, and the Midrashic Literature</u>
(1903; repr. Judaica Press, New York, 1971).
J. Levy, <u>Neuhebräisches und chaldäisches
Wörterbuch</u> (Brockhaus, Leipzig, 1876-1889) 4 vols.
(repr. Wissenschaftliche Buchgesellschaft,
Darmstadt).
E. Vogt (ed.), <u>Lexicon Linguae Aramaicae Veteris</u>

Testamenti Documentis Antiquis Illustratum
(Pontifical Biblical Institute, Rome, 1971).

3. Qumran Literature

No standard work on the dialects of Qumran is
yet available, although there are several studies of
particular aspects. See E.Y. Kutscher in
Encyclopaedia Judaica, vol. 16, cols. 1583-1590 for
a summary. See further sec. 22 below and Milik's
edition of the Enoch fragments (sec. 21.5 below).
This is important for Gospel criticism, and some
Qumran material has been used in M. Black, An
Aramaic Approach to the Gospels and Acts[3] (Clarendon
Press, Oxford, 1967). (Black's book is important
for the relevance of Aramaic study to the NT in
general; but see the critical review by J.A.
Fitzmyer, CBQ 30 (1968) 417-428.)

4. The Language(s) of Jesus

The debate as to which language(s) Jesus is
likely to have spoken is still continuing. M. Black
gave a useful survey of the state of the question in
In Memoriam Paul Kahle, ed. M. Black & G. Fohrer
(Töpelmann, Berlin, 1968) 17-28. Fuller and more
recent is J.A. Fitzmyer, 'The Languages of Palestine
in the First Century AD', CBQ 32 (1970) 501-531. Cf
also C. Rabin in Corpus Rerum Iudaicarum I/2 (see
sec. 12 above), 1007-1039, with special bibliography
on the language of Jesus.

5. Bibliography

For sections 16 and 17 see J.H. Hospers (ed.),
A Basic Bibliography for the Study of the Semitic
Languages, vol. 1, (E.J. Brill, Leiden, 1973),
covering all Semitic and other Ancient Near Eastern
languages, except Arabic, which is dealt with in
vol. 2.

18. THE TARGUMS

The Targums are Aramaic versions of the OT, commenced in the Exilic period or soon after, which can provide material for general background, for OT interpretation, and esp. for the question of Aramaic substrata in the NT.

The oldest extant MSS are of Job and Leviticus, found at Qumran: see J.P.M. Van der Ploeg & A.S. Van der Woude, Le Targum de Job de la Grotte XI de Qumrân (E.J. Brill, Leiden, 1971) and J.T. Milik, DJD VI (see sec. 22) 86-90. All other Targum texts are derived from mediaeval copies (7th century AD and later), and their age can be judged only on subjective grounds, which limits their usefulness to some degree. New material, some of it still unpublished, complicates the obscure history of the various Targums.

M. Black (see sec. 17.3) has surveyed the situation up to January 1967. More details are given in M. MacNamara, The NT and the Palestinian Targum (Biblical Institute Press, Rome, 1966). A useful article by G.J. Cowling on the Palestinian Targum and its relevance to the NT, with bibliography, appeared in TSF Bulletin 51 (1968) 6-15; he disputes the early date frequently proposed.

A useful introduction to the Targums as a whole, and their relevance to NT study, with details of all extant Targums, is M. MacNamara, Targum and Testament (Irish UP, Shannon, 1972). See also R. Le Deaut, Introduction a la Littérature Targumique (Biblical Institute Press, Rome, 1966).

The standard text of the Babylonian Targums (Onkelos on the Pentateuch, Jonathan on the Prophets) is A. Sperber, The Bible in Aramaic (E. J. Brill, Leiden, 1959-73) 5 vols. B. Walton, Biblia Sacra Polyglotta (London, 1657) gives texts and Latin translations.

English translations:-

J.W. Etheridge, <u>The Targums of Onkelos and
Jonathan ben Uzziel on the Pentateuch with the
Fragments of the Jerusalem Targum</u> (1862-5, 2 vols;
repr. in 1 vol., Ktav, New York, 1968) - 'Jonathan
ben Uzziel' = the Palestinian Targum, sometimes
called 'Pseudo-Jonathan'.
J.F. Stenning, <u>The Targum of Isaiah</u> (Clarendon
Press, Oxford, 1949) - pointed text, with transla-
tion.
J. Bowker, <u>The Targums and Rabbinic Literature</u>
(Cambridge UP, 1969) includes a translation of much
of Pseudo-Jonathan on Genesis.
The 5-volume edition of <u>Neophyti I</u> by A. Diez
Macho (Consejo Superior de Investigaciones
Cientificas, Madrid/Barcelona, 1968-1978) contains
English trans.

P. Nickels, <u>Targum and NT</u> (Biblical Institute
Press, Rome, 1967) lists works old and new which use
the Targums in elucidating the text and exegesis of
the NT, giving a detailed index, verse by verse, of
NT passages which have been explained in relation to
targumic literature, with bibliography.

For full bibliography see B. Grossfeld, <u>A
Bibliography of Targum Literature</u> (Ktav, New York
1972), covering literature from the sixteenth
century to 1971, with some descriptive comments.

19. <u>THE SEPTUAGINT</u>

Most surviving copies of the Septuagint (LXX)
are the work of Christian scribes. Qumran and other
discoveries throw fresh light on recensional
problems. Brief accounts of the several recensions
(e.g. Theodotion, Lucian) and of other Greek versions
(Aquila, Symmachus) can be found in standard textual
histories, e.g. F.G. Kenyon, <u>The Text of the Greek
Bible</u>, 3rd ed., revised A.W. Adams (Duckworth,
London, 1975). For LXX textual criticism see P.
Walters, <u>The Text of the Septuagint: Its Corruptions
and their Emendations</u>, ed. D.W. Gooding (Cambridge

UP, 1973).

The most useful introduction to LXX studies in general is S. Jellicoe, <u>The Septuagint and Modern Study</u> (Oxford UP, 1968, repr. Eisenbraun, Ann Arbor, 1978). H.B. Swete, <u>An Introduction to the OT in Greek</u> (2nd ed. ed. R.R. Ottley, Cambridge UP, 1914, repr. Ktav, New York) still contains much of value to the NT student. See also the collection of essays, <u>Studies in the Septuagint: Origins, Recensions and Interpretations</u>, ed. S. Jellicoe (Ktav, New York, 1974).

The standard <u>text</u> is <u>A. Rahlfs, Septuaginta</u> (Württembergische Bibelanstalt, Stuttgart, 1935) 2 vols. Also often used is H.B. Swete, <u>The Old Testament in Greek</u> (Cambridge UP, 1887-1902) 4 vols, with a full introduction. There are two major critical editions:-

A.E. Brooks & N. McLean, <u>The OT in Greek</u> (Cambridge UP, 1906-1940) 9 vols. Covers Pentateuch, historical books, Esther, Judith, Tobit only. ('The Larger Cambridge').
The Göttingen LXX (Vandenhoeck & Ruprecht, Göttingen, 1931-   ) 14 vols. to date, viz. Genesis; Deut; Esther; 1 Esdras; 1 Macc; 2 & 3 Macc; Psalms & Odes; Wisdom; Sirach; Minor Prophets; Is; Jer, Baruch, Lam & Ep. Jer; Ezek; Dan, Sus & Bel. (This is a synthetic text, not representing particular manuscripts as the Cambridge editions do.)

The remaining fragments of the cther Greek versions and recensions are still most conveniently found in F. Field, <u>Origenis Hexaplorum quae Supersunt ...</u> (Clarendon Press, Oxford, 1875) 2 vols.

The standard concordance is E. Hatch & H.A. Redpath, <u>A Concordance to the Septuagint and the other Greek versions of the OT</u> (Clarendon Press, Oxford, 1897) 2 vols., and supp. with proper names and Hebrew index (1906); the whole reprinted Graz, 1954. Note also E.C. Dos Santos, <u>An Expanded Hebrew Index for the Hatch-Redpath Concordance to the Septuagint</u> (Dugith, Jerusalem, 1973) for a listing

of the Greek words used by the LXX for each Hebrew
word.
   X. Jacques, <u>List of Septuagint Words sharing Common
Elements</u> (Biblical Institute Press, Rome, 1972)
provides the same valuable help as his companion
volume for the NT (see sec. 7 above).

   Some idea of the treatment of the Massoretic
text by the LXX can be gained from D.W. Gooding's
<u>Relics of Ancient Exegesis</u> (Cambridge UP, 1976) and
esp. his article in <u>Textus</u> 7 (1969) 1-29.

20. <u>THE INTER-TESTAMENTAL PERIOD</u>

   For the Jewish literature of this period, see
secs. 21 and 22 below. The history and religious
development of the period is covered in many of the
standard histories of Israel. NB esp. F.F. Bruce,
<u>Israel and the Nations</u> (Paternoster, London, 1963),
the bulk of which deals with the period from the
Exile to AD 70.

   A basic introduction to this period is D.S.
Russell, <u>The Jews from Alexander to Herod</u> (Clarendon
Bible, Oxford, 1967). For a more recent and fuller
treatment see D.E. Gowan, <u>Bridge between the
Testaments</u> (Pickwick Press, Pittsburgh, 1976). The
first half of R.H. Pfeiffer, <u>A History of NT Times</u>,
with an Introduction to the Apocrypha (A. & C.
Black, London, 1949) covers Judaism from 200 BC to
AD 200 from a radical critical point of view. Cf
also the works listed in sec. 12 above for historical
background to NT history.

   For further bibliography, see the relevant
articles in e.g. <u>NBD</u> or <u>IDB</u>, and also Delling's
<u>Bibliographie</u> mentioned in sec. 24 below.

   The following more specialised works are of
particular value for reference:

   E. Schürer, <u>A History of the Jewish People in the</u>

Time of Christ (ET, T. & T. Clark, Edinburgh, from 1895) 5 vols. and index vol. A standard work, on a massive scale, covering the period from 175 BC to AD 135, from the political, social, religious, and literary points of view. A completely revised and updated English version is now being published, under the editorship of M. Black, G. Vermes, and F. Millar: vol. 1 (T. & T. Clark, Edinburgh, 1973) covers the political history; vol. 2 due 1979; vol. 3 in preparation.

J. Jeremias, _Jerusalem in the Time of Jesus_ (ET, London, 1969). A study of life in Jerusalem, in economic and social terms, in great detail. Much valuable incidental information.

M. Hengel, _Judaism and Hellenism_ (ET, SCM, London, 1974) 2 vols. A massive study, with full bibliography, of the cultural and religious tensions in Palestine from Alexander to the Maccabees.

W. Bousset, _Die Religion des Judentums im NT Zeitalter_, ed. H. Gressmann (J.C.B. Mohr, Tübingen, 1966). From the Maccabees to Hadrian.

ME!

21. THE OLD TESTAMENT APOCRYPHA AND PSEUDEPIGRAPHA

1. Introductions ~~Ps of Solomon~~

The most convenient general introduction to the material as a whole is O. Eissfeldt, _The OT, an Introduction_ (ET, Blackwell, Oxford, 1965), pp. 571-637, containing a brief introduction and full bibliography for each book. For the Pseudepigrapha see also A.-M. Denis, _Introduction aux Pseudepigraphes Grecs d'AT_ (E.J. Brill, Leiden, 1970); very detailed. More briefly, L. Rost, _Einleitung in die alttestamentlichen Apokryphen and Pseudepigraphen_ (Quelle & Meyer, Heidelberg, 1971). For the apocalyptic works see also D.S. Russell, _The Method and Message of Jewish Apocalyptic_ (SCM, London, 1964), and more briefly, L. Morris, _Apocalyptic_ (IVP, London, 1973).

For the Apocrypha see also:-

B.M. Metzger, <u>An Introduction to the Apocrypha</u>
(Oxford UP, New York, 1957).
L.H. Brockington, <u>A Critical Introduction to the
Apocrypha</u> (Duckworth, London, 1961).

2. Bibliography

In addition to the bibliographies in the above
introductions (esp. Eissfeldt and Denis) see:

G. Delling, <u>Bibliographie zur jüdisch-
hellenistischen und intertestamentarischen Literatur
1900-1970</u> (Akademie-Verlag, Berlin, 1975).
J.H. Charlesworth, <u>The Pseudepigrapha and Modern
Research</u> (Scholars Press, Missoula, Montana, 1976),
with a comprehensive coverage of the vastly
increasing scholarly output in this area in recent
years (since 1960); designed to be used in conjunc-
tion with Delling, but more immediately helpful for
the non-specialist.

3. Texts and Translations

The Greek texts of the books of the Apocrypha
will be found in a good edition of the LXX (see sec.
19). For the Pseudepigrapha, the text is best
found in editions of the individual books: for
details, see Eissfeldt, etc. Two new series of
Greek texts of the OT Pseudepigrapha are now in
publication:

<u>Pseudepigrapha Veteris Testamenti Graece</u> (E.J.
Brill, Leiden): so far, M. de Jonge, <u>Testamenta XII
Patriarcharum</u> (1964); S. Brock, <u>Testamentum Iobi</u>
with J.C. Picard, <u>Apocalypsis Baruchi</u> (1967); M.
Black, <u>Apocalypsis Henochi</u> with A.-M. Denis,
<u>Fragmenta Pseudepigraphorum</u> (1970); O. Wahl,
<u>Apocalypsis Esdrae, Apocalypsis Sedrach, Visio Beati
Esdrae</u> (1977).
<u>Texts and Translations, Pseudepigrapha Series</u>
(Scholars Press, Missoula, Montana, from 1972)
contains original texts in Greek and other languages.

In English, most of the important books are
collected in R.H. Charles (ed.) <u>The Apocrypha and
Pseudepigrapha of the OT</u> (Clarendon Press, Oxford,
1913; repr. 1963) 2 huge vols. The introductory
material in Charles is still one of the most
convenient collections on the Pseudepigrapha.

A new collection of all the important
Pseudepigrapha (in English translation, with notes)
ed. H.F.D. Sparks (Clarendon Press, Oxford), is
'nearly finished' according to Charlesworth, 1976.
A more comprehensive collection of English translations (ed. J.H. Charlesworth) is also in hand,
published by Doubleday, New York.

4. Concordance

C.A. Wahl, <u>Clavis Librorum Veteris Testamenti
Apocryphorum</u> (1853) was a lexicon-cum-concordance of
the Apocrypha. Superseded as a concordance by Hatch
and Redpath (see sec. 19), but in the reprint by
Akademische Druck- und Verlagsanstalt, Graz (1972)
there are also included new concordances (ed. J.B.
Bauer) to some of the major Greek <u>pseudepigrapha</u>,
individually, and references (p. 512) to existing
concordances to other pseudepigrapha.

5. Editions and Commentaries

Again, see the introductions and bibliographies
for details. Many of the older large-scale editions
have not yet been adequately replaced, but modern
scholarship is steadily filling the gaps.

Many of these books have appeared at Qumran, so
that it is often valuable to consult books on the
Qumran literature (see sec. 22) in this connection.
Estimates of the Book of Enoch have been particularly affected. See the new edition by J.T. Milik,
<u>The Books of Enoch: Aramaic Fragments from Qumrân
Cave 4</u> (Clarendon Press, Oxford, 1976), with
exhaustive discussion.

22. QUMRAN

The literature is voluminous, and constantly increasing. Much of the earlier work was premature, and is now outdated.

1. General Introductions

These are many, and disagree among themselves, even on essential matters. The following earlier accounts give the basic facts, and a fair range of possible interpretation:

F.M. Cross, Jr., The Ancient Library of Qumran (Duckworth, London, 1958).
J.T. Milik, Ten Years of Discovery in the Wilderness of Judaea (ET, SCM, London, 1959).

Each of these works gives the standard abbreviations for the individual texts (1QM, etc.)

A more recent assessment is G. Vermes, The Dead Sea Scrolls: Qumran in Perspective (Collins, London, 1977), with useful subject-bibliographies, and a guide to editions of the texts.

2. Texts

The major edition, in the process of publication, is:

Discoveries in the Judaean Desert (Clarendon Press, Oxford). (Abbrev. DJD) To date: Vol. I (1955) Cave 1 fragments; Vol. II (1960) Murabba'at; Vol. III (1962) Caves 2-3, 5-10; Vol. IV (1965) Cave 11 Psalm Scroll (a further fragment of this scroll was published by Y. Yadin, Textus 5 (1966) 1-10); Vol. V (1968) Cave 4 biblical commentaries (supplemented by a bibliographical article by J.A. Fitzmyer, CBQ 31 (1969) 59-71, and by a very important study by J. Strugnell in Revue de Qumran 7.2 (1970) 163-276); Vol. VI (1977) Cave 4 Tefillin, Mezuzot and Targums. Further volumes are planned to contain the remaining

Cave 4 texts.

Primary publications of the major Cave 1 texts are as follows:

M. Burrows, The Dead Sea Scrolls of St. Mark's Monastery (American Schools of Oriental Research, New Haven), vol. 1 (1950) 1QIsaA and 1QpHab; vol. 2 (1951) 1QS. The original colour photographs of these texts are available in J.C. Trever, Scrolls from Qumran Cave I (Albright Institute of Archaeological Research, Jerusalem, 1972).
E.L. Sukenik, The Dead Sea Scrolls of the Hebrew University (Magnes Press, Jerusalem, 1955) 1QIsaB, 1QM, 1QH.
N. Avigad & Y. Yadin, A Genesis Apocryphon (Magnes Press, Jerusalem, 1956).
Y. Yadin, The Temple Scroll (Israel Exploration Society, Jerusalem, 1977 - in Hebrew, ET in press).

Other primary publications are listed in Milik (above) pp. 147-149, and in Kuhn's Konkordanz (below) pp. V-VII. For a complete list to 1967 see J.A. Sanders, 'Palestinian Manuscripts, 1947-1967' JBL 86 (1967) 431-440.

E. Lohse, Die Texte aus Qumran[2] (Kösel, München, 1971) gives a pointed Hebrew text of the main non-biblical MSS of Caves 1 and 4, with German translation and brief notes.

English Translations of the main texts are found in:

T.H. Gaster, The Scriptures of the Dead Sea Sect (Secker and Warburg, London, 1957) - often rather too free.
G. Vermes, The Dead Sea Scrolls in English[2] (Penguin, 1975).

NB It is not wise to use one of these translations alone, as they differ radically both in reconstruction and translation of the texts.

3. Editions and Commentaries on Individual Texts

The series 'Studies on the Texts of the Desert of Judah' (E.J. Brill, Leiden) includes commentaries on 1QS (P. Wernberg-Møller, 1957); 1QM (J. Van der Ploeg, 1959); 1QH (M. Mansoor, 1961).

Among other editions the following are important:

C. Rabin, The Zadokite Documents[2] (Clarendon Press, Oxford, 1958).

Y. Yadin, The Scroll of the War ... (ET, Oxford UP, 1962).

A.R.C. Leaney, The Rule of Qumran and its Meaning (SCM, London, 1966).

J.A. Fitzmyer, The Genesis Apocryphon of Qumran Cave 1[2] (Biblical Institute Press, Rome, 1971).

Chapter 3 of Vermes, The Dead Sea Scrolls (sec. 1 above) provides an up-to-date guide to editions available.

4. Concordance

K.G. Kuhn, Konkordanz zu den Qumrantexten (Vandenhoeck & Ruprecht, Göttingen, 1960) lists all Hebrew words in non-biblical texts published up to 1960, including the Damascus Document. Supplement in Revue de Qumran 4 (1963) 163-234.

5. Bibliographies

Revue de Qumran, published in Paris since 1958, contains important articles, statistical material, and reviews. It also has a complete running bibliography of 'scientific' articles and books in the field of Qumran studies published since 1957.

See also B. Jongeling, A Classified Bibliography of the Finds in the Desert of Judah, 1958-1969 (E.J. Brill, Leiden, 1971); J.A. Fitzmyer, The Dead Sea Scrolls: Major Publications and Tools for Study (Scholars Press, Missoula, Montana, 1975).

For bibliography of earlier publications, see
C. Burchard, <u>Bibliographie zu den Handschriften vom
toten Meer</u> (Töpelmann, Berlin, 1957); there is also
a second volume, published 1965. Also W.S. LaSor,
<u>Bibliography of the Dead Sea Scrolls, 1948-1957</u>
(Fuller Theological Seminary, Pasadena, Calif., 1958;
= <u>Fuller Library Bulletin</u> 31).

See also M. Yizhar, <u>Bibliography of Hebrew
Publications on the Dead Sea Scrolls (1948-1964)</u>
(Harvard UP, Cambridge, Mass., 1967).

6. <u>Some Other Useful Publications</u>

A.S. Van der Woude, <u>Die messianischen Vorstellungen
der Gemeinde von Qumran</u> (Van Gorcum, Assen, 1957).
Much useful exegetical material.
K. Stendahl (ed.), <u>The Scrolls and the NT</u> (SCM,
London, 1958) brings together articles of varying
value from the earlier days of Qumran studies.
G.R. Driver, <u>The Judaean Scrolls</u> (Blackwell,
Oxford, 1965). A massive, if eccentric, treatment,
full of information, invaluable for references,
indices, etc. Driver's conclusions, however, are not
widely accepted.
H. Braun, <u>Qumran und das NT</u> (J.C.B. Mohr, Tübingen,
1966) 2 vols. The first part includes critical
surveys of the literature on specific subjects (e.g.
John the Baptist and Qumran); the second part
discusses the literature on individual NT passages
on which Qumran is alleged to throw some light. Cf
the same author's <u>Spätjüdisch-häretischer und
frühchristlicher Radikalismus</u> (J.C.B. Mohr, Tübingen,
1957) 2 vols., comparing Pirqe Aboth, the Qumran
texts, and the Synoptic Gospels.
J.H. Charlesworth (ed.), <u>John and Qumran</u> (Chapman,
London, 1972). A collection of essays bringing
together some widely accepted results of study in
this area.
W.S. LaSor, <u>The Dead Sea Scrolls and the NT</u>
(Eerdmans, Grand Rapids, 1972). An attempt to
separate solid results and reasonable possibilities
from sensational claims.

23. PHILO AND JOSEPHUS

Frequently referred to in NT studies, as they are the two major Hellenistic Jewish writers of the NT period. Their works are most conveniently consulted in the Loeb edition (see sec. 26) - Philo, ed. F.H. Colson, G.H. Whitaker & R. Marcus, 12 vols. (1929-1953); Josephus, ed. H.St J. Thackeray, R. Marcus & L.H. Feldman, 9 vols. (1926-1965).

For an introduction to Philo, see E.R. Goodenough, An Introduction to Philo Judaeus[2] (Blackwell, Oxford, 1962). Also Schürer (see sec. 20 above) section 34 (old ed. vol. II/iii, pp. 321-381; new ed. not yet available). For Josephus, see H.St J. Thackeray, Josephus, the Man and the Historian (Jewish Institute of Religion, New York, 1929); more recent, and conveniently brief, is R.J.H. Shutt, Studies in Josephus (SPCK, London, 1961).

For a concordance to the works of Philo see G. Mayer, Index Philoneus (de Gruyter, Berlin, 1974). For Josephus, A Complete Concordance to Flavius Josephus, ed. K.H. Rengstorf is being published by E.J. Brill, Leiden. Vols. 1 and 2 (1973, 1975) cover A to K; a Supplement (1968) contains a concordance to proper names by A. Schalit. Parts I-IV (covering A to E) of A Lexicon to Flavius Josephus by H.St J. Thackeray & R. Marcus were published by P. Geuthner, Paris, 1930-1955; it was never completed.

Bibliography will be found in L.H. Feldman, Scholarship on Philo and Josephus (1937-1962) (Studies in Judaica, Yeshiva Univ., New York, n.d.). For more recent work see E. Hilgert, A Bibliography of Philo Studies 1963-1970, and Abstracts of Selected Articles on Philo 1966-1970, both in Studia Philonica 1 (1972) 57-91. (This will now be the key journal for Philo studies.) For Josephus see also H. Schreckenberg, Bibliographie zu Flavius Josephus (E.J. Brill, Leiden, 1968).

24. JUDAISM AND RABBINIC LITERATURE

1. Reference Works on Judaism

Encyclopaedia Judaica, ed. C. Roth (Keter, Jerusalem, 1971) 16 vols.

The Jewish Encyclopaedia, I. Singer (Funk & Wagnall, New York/London, 1901-1906) 12 vols. Now generally superseded by the above, but still worth consulting on specific points.

G.F. Moore, Judaism in the First Centuries of the Christian Era (Harvard UP, 1927-1930) 3 vols. Still of great value, despite some severe criticism; nothing comparable has replaced it.

E. Schürer, A History of the Jewish People in the Time of Christ - see sec. 20.

J. Neusner, Rabbinic Traditions about the Pharisees before 70 (E. J. Brill, Leiden, 1971) 3 vols. A major contribution to the study of the Rabbinic authorities of the NT period; radical and contro-versial. NB esp. the 'Bibliographical Reflections' (vol. 3, pp. 320-368) fpr some stringent criticisms of much previous work, as well as bibliographical help.

T. Reinach, Textes d'Auteurs Grecs et Romains relatifs au Judaisme (Paris, 1895). Useful for source material, but now being replaced by M. Stern, Greek and Latin Authors on Jews and Judaism (Israel Academy of Sciences and Humanities, Jerusalem). Vol. 1 (1974) covers from Herodotus to Plutarch.

E.R. Goodenough, Jewish Symbols in the Graeco-Roman Period (Pantheon, New York, 1953-1968) 13 vols. A monumental and sumptuous work on religious symbolism in archaeological material and in literature.

2. Bibliographies

Index of Articles on Jewish Studies, published annually since 1969 by Magnes Press, Jerusalem. Each issue covers the publications of three years previously (i.e. 1973 issue covers articles published in 1970, etc.).

C. Berlin, Index to Festschriften in Jewish Studies (Ktav, New York, 1971).

J. Neusner (ed.) <u>The Study of Judaism:</u>
<u>Bibliographical Essays</u> (Ktav, New York, 1972).
  See also G. Delling in sec. 21.2 above, and the
bibliographies in Schürer (sec. 20 above) vol. 1, pp.
68-118.

3. Introductions to Rabbinic Literature

  H.L. Strack, <u>Introduction to the Talmud and</u>
<u>Midrash</u> (ET, Jewish Publication Society,
Philadelphia, 1931; repr. Atheneum, New York, 1969).
Very stodgy, consisting mainly of lists of Rabbis and
their writings; but comprehensive, and an essential
tool when confronted by weird titles and enigmatic
abbreviations!
  J. Bowker, <u>The Targums and Rabbinic Literature</u>
(Cambridge UP, 1969). Provides a more readable
general description of the literature.
  C. Albeck, <u>Einführung in die Mischna</u> (de Gruyter,
Berlin, 1971). The most up-to-date work on the
Mishnah alone.

  Perhaps the most convenient general introduction is now the new ed. of Schürer (see sec. 20),
vol. 1, pp. 68-118.

  For linguistic aids, see above secs. 16 and 17.

4. The Literature Itself

  Rabbinic literature may be divided into two
main classes, Talmud and Midrash.

  (a) <u>Talmud</u>. The basis of the Talmud is the
Mishnah, collected sayings of Rabbis compiled c AD
200. It is reasonably brief, but obscurely concise.
A pointed Hebrew text with English translation and
notes is P. Blackman, <u>Mishnayoth</u> (Mishna Press,
London, 1951-1956) 7 vols. The most convenient
English edition is H. Danby, <u>The Mishnah</u> (Oxford UP,
1933). The Mishnah is divided into six Orders
(Sedarim), each of which is divided into a number of
Tractates, 63 in all.

Further material of the same period makes up the Tosephta, compiled slightly later, with the same arrangement of Orders and Tractates. The standard edition is <u>Tosephta</u>, ed. M.S. Zuckermandel, with supplement by S. Liebermann (Bamberger & Wahrmann, Jerusalem, 1937). An English translation was begun in 1977, ed. J. Neusner, <u>The Tosefta: vol. 6: Tohorot</u> (Ktav, New York, 1977); <u>vol. 5: Qodoshim</u> (1979); 4 vols. to follow. A German translation and commentary (ed. K.H. Rengstorf) is being published by Kohlhammer, Stuttgart, since 1960.

The Talmud consists of Mishnah + Gemara (i.e. expository material arising out of the Mishnah, and is arranged according to the Tractates of the Mishnah. There are two extant talmudic collections, the Babylonian (completed early sixth century AD) and the Palestinian (early fifth century). The former is much longer, and is the one generally referred to. The Hebrew-Aramaic text, with German translation, may be found in L. Goldschmidt (ed.), <u>Der babylonische Talmud</u> (Berlin, Leipzig, Hague, 1897-1935) 9 vols. For English translation see I. Epstein (ed.), <u>The Babylonian Talmud</u> (Soncino Press, London, 1935-1952) 35 vols., reprinted in 18 vols. 1961. There is also a uniform edition of the extra-canonical tractates (including the important <u>Aboth D'Rabbi Nathan</u>): A. Cohen (ed.), <u>The Minor Tractates of the Talmud</u> (Soncino, London, 1965) 2 vols. Soncino Press are now in process of publishing the Babylonian Talmud in Hebrew with English translation; 10 Tractates published to date (not in talmudic order). The Palestinian Talmud is most conveniently found in the French translation by M. Schwab, <u>Le Talmud de Jérusalem</u> (Paris, 1871-1890; repr. 1960 in 6 vols.); there is no complete English translation, but for a few tractates published in English and German see Schürer vol. 1 p. 84.

(b) <u>Midrash</u>. The midrashim are extended commentaries on the books of the OT. For full details see, e.g. Strack's <u>Introduction</u>. The 'Tannaitic' Midrashim (of the period of the Mishnah roughly) are the oldest; they are Mekilta on Exodus, Sifra on Lev., Sifre on Num. and Dt. The only full

English translation is of Mekilta, ed. J.Z.
Lauterbach (Jewish Publication Society, New York,
1933-1935, paperback reprint 1976) 3 vols. Mekilta
was also published in German, ed. J. Winter and A.
Wünsche (Leipzig, 1909), and Sifre Num. also in
German, ed. K.G. Kuhn (Kohlhammer, Stuttgart, 1959).
Selections from Sifre Num. in English are found in
P.P. Levertoff, Midrash Sifre on Numbers (SPCK,
London, 1926). See also the extracts in Bonsirven's
collection, below.

The most important of the later midrashim are
the collection known as Midrash Rabbah, of various
dates, covering the Pentateuch and the Five
Megilloth; published in English, ed. H. Freedman &
M. Simon (Soncino Press, London, 1939) 10 vols. Two
other convenient English versions of important
midrashim are published by Yale UP, New Haven, and
edited by W.G. Braude, The Midrash on Psalms (1959)
2 vols; Pesikta Rabbati (1969) 2 vols.

The student who has got this far will be in a
position to find his own way through the intricacies
of the other midrashim!

5. Systems of Reference and Abbreviation

The Rabbinic texts most commonly referred to are
the Mishnah, the Babylonian Talmud, and the Midrash
Rabbah. Other references, not here explained, are
usually clear on consulting the relevant text. (See
further the useful list of abbreviations in Jastrow's
Dictionary (above sec. 17) pp. XV-XVIII.)

No system of reference is universally accepted;
the following are the most common in English
writings:-

References to the Mishnah are by Tractate (sometimes preceded by M), with two figures following,
representing section and subsection. Those to the
Babylonian Talmud are by Tractate (sometimes preceded
by B), with a figure and a letter following (representing the folio of the standard ed. of 1520: a

indicates one side of the sheet, b the other - all later editions mark these divisions). Thus Ber. 3.2 = Mishnah, Tractate Berakoth 3.2; Ber. 3b = Babylonian Talmud, Tractate Berakoth, 3b.

References to the <u>Palestinian Talmud</u> are by Tractate, preceded by P, J or Y, and may be either by section or by folio, or both; thus, P Taan 4.5 (68d).

References to the <u>Midrash Rabbah</u> are indicated by the name of the biblical book followed by R (thus Gen R; or sometimes using the abbreviated Hebrew name of the book, Ber. R). References follow two systems: for the Pentateuch, Ruth and Esther, the midrash is divided into section and subsection without reference to the passage of the OT under discussion; thus Gen R 3.2 = Midrash Rabbah on Genesis, section 3, subsection 2 (<u>not</u> Midrash Rabbah on Gen. 3.2 - this passage is not in fact discussed until Gen R 19.3). For Lam., Eccles. and Song the reference <u>is</u> to the biblical verse or group of verses under discussion; the discussion of each verse or group is generally subdivided, and a further figure indicates the paragraph; thus Lam R 2.2 para 4, or Lam R 3.5-8 para 2.

6. Collections of Rabbinic Material

H.L. Strack & P. Billerbeck, <u>Kommentar zum NT aus Talmud und Midrasch</u> (Beck, München, 1922-1928; vols. V and VI, 1956-1961) is indispensable. Vols. I-III go through the NT verse by verse, citing wherever possible material from the whole range of Rabbinic and other Jewish literature (including Targums and Pseudepigrapha) to illustrate the passage. The relevant material is quoted in full, in German. Vol. IV (published in two parts) consists of lengthy excursuses on the commentary, with general index and index of Scripture references. Vol. V (by J. Jeremias and K. Adolph) is an index of all Rabbinic and other passages cited in vols. I-IV. Vol. VI (by the same authors) is a very useful list of the Rabbis whose sayings occur in the passages cited,

with their dates, and index of citations; charts at
the back set out their relationship with one another
as teacher, pupil, etc. There is also an index of
places. (Abbrev. SB; sometimes referred to as
'Billerbeck'.)

C.G. Montefiore. Rabbinic Literature and Gospel
Teachings (Macmillan, London, 1930). A poor
Englishman's SB! Cites Rabbinic passages relevant
to Mt. and Lk. only.

C.G. Montefiore & H. Loewe, A Rabbinic Anthology
(Macmillan, London, 1938). Much fuller and more
valuable, but not directly related to the NT.
Arranged by subjects.

J. Bonsirven (ed.), Textes Rabbiniques des Deux
Premiers Siècles Chrétiens pour servir a
l'Intelligence du NT (Pontifical Biblical Institute,
Rome, 1955). Does what the title says. Being
restricted to the early period, it consists largely
of extracts from the Mishnah and both talmudic
collections, with useful material from the Tannaitic
Midrashim. Long and useful subject index, and index
of NT passages to which the extracts are relevant.

J. Lightfoot, A Commentary on the NT from the
Talmud and Hebraica (Baker, Grand Rapids, 1979) is a
four-volume reprint of a 19th century English
translation of a 17th century Latin 'equivalent' to
SB.

7. Some Important Works Relating Rabbinic Material to
   the NT

J. Bowker, Jesus and the Pharisees (Cambridge UP,
1973). Brings conveniently together material from
Jewish sources illustrating or relating to Jesus'
conflict with the establishment.

D. Daube, The NT and Rabbinic Judaism (Athlone
Press, London, 1956).

W.D. Davies, Paul and Rabbinic Judaism [2] (SPCK,
London, 1955). Most of Davies' books are helpful in
this field; The Setting of the Sermon on the Mount
(Cambridge UP, 1964) is full of valuable detailed
information.

J.W. Doeve, Jewish Hermeneutics in the Synoptic
Gospels and Acts (Van Gorcum, Assen, 1954). An

interesting, if not always convincing, attempt to trace Rabbinic methods of exegesis in the NT.

B. Gerhardsson, Memory and Manuscript, Oral Tradition and Written Transmission in Rabbinic Judaism and Early Christianity (Uppsala, 1961); pp. 19-189 give an invaluable insight into Jewish ideas on tradition, teaching, etc. An important book, even if he does overplay his hand in tracing similar ideas and practices in the NT. (NB W.D. Davies' review, an appendix in The Setting of the Sermon on the Mount, and Gerhardsson's reply to this and other reviews in his Tradition and Transmission in Early Christianity (Gleerup, Lund, 1964).

E.P. Sanders, Paul and Palestinian Judaism (SCM, London, 1977). A detailed study of Judaism as seen in tannaitic literature, Qumran, Apocrypha and Pseudepigrapha, with trenchant criticism of much previous work. Helpful bibliography and guide to systems of reference.

S. Sandmel, Judaism and Christian Beginnings (OUP, New York, 1978). The refreshing non-technical work of a Jewish scholar thoroughly at home in NT studies with their frequent misuse of Jewish material.

8. Comments and Cautions

The NT scholar needs to approach Rabbinics with a due sense of his lack of expertise in this field. The whole approach to learning, argument, exegesis, etc. is so totally different from that of the NT that he needs an orientation course. The first part of Gerhardsson's Memory and Manuscript might help to provide this; or G. Vermes, Scripture and Tradition in Judaism[2] (E.J. Brill, Leiden, 1973), a useful study of Rabbinic exegesis and haggadic development.

Caution is particularly necessary in the dating of a given piece of teaching. A careful use of SB vol. VI will help in this. H. Loewe discusses the question in A Rabbinic Anthology (see above) pp. 694-737, giving similar lists of Rabbis, and dates for the extracts in the Anthology. It is often impossible to tell whether a saying attributed to a given Rabbi may not be derived from a predecessor,

and where there is no attribution, a reliable dating
is virtually impossible. The NT student must
remember the effects of the events of AD 70 on
Jewish thought, before attempting to read views back
into the NT period from later material.

It is usually advisable to avoid generalisations
about 'the Rabbinic teaching' on a subject - the
material is vast, and it is not unlikely that a
contradictory view will be expressed elsewhere,
perhaps side by side with its opposite!

25. EARLY CHRISTIAN AND GNOSTIC LITERATURE

This is a vast field, of much more importance
to NT studies than is generally recognised in
Britain. German scholarship, however, has not been
slow to recognise the importance of second century
literature for our understanding of the history and
theology of the early church, including the NT
period. See esp. W. Bauer, Orthodoxy and Heresy in
Earliest Christianity (ET, SCM, London, 1972): a
mine of information in this area.

(1) New Testament Apocrypha

E. Hennecke, NT Apocrypha (ed. W. Schneemelcher;
ET ed. R. McL. Wilson, Lutterworth Press, London,
vol. 1, 1963; vol. 2, 1965; reprinted by SCM Press,
London, 1973 and 1974) provides good introductions,
up-to-date bibliographies, and translations of
virtually all the texts of any importance for NT
studies. This will be the standard work for a long
time to come. The range of material included in the
two vols. is enormous, from material relevant to the
history of the NT canon, and extra-canonical sayings
of Jesus, to Gnostic Gospels.

(2) Nag Hammadi and Other Gnostic Literature

Many NT scholars contend that the discovery at

Nag Hammadi in 1948 of a large collection of Gnostic documents (in Coptic) may eventually prove to be at least as important for NT studies as the Qumran finds.

The standard ed. is <u>The Facsimile Edition of the Nag Hammadi Codices</u> (E.J. Brill, Leiden, 1972-1977); 10 vols. Earlier publications of the texts are listed in the Introduction to this series. The complete contents in English translation are published in J.M. Robinson (ed.), <u>The Nag Hammadi Library in English</u> (E.J. Brill, Leiden, 1977).

The best guide to the whole field is <u>Le Origini dello Gnosticismo</u>: Colloquio di Messina, 1966, ed. U. Bianchi (E.J. Brill, Leiden, 1967). Includes papers and discussions (in English, French, German and Italian) from the 1966 conference. Articles on the definition and origin of Gnosticism, on the standard eds. of the texts, and on the relationship of the field to the NT are useful. See also:

A.K. Helmbold, <u>The Nag Hammadi Gnostic Texts and the Bible</u> (Baker, Grand Rapids, 1967). Helpful introductory survey; good bibliographies.

R. McL. Wilson, <u>Gnosis and the NT</u> (Blackwell, Oxford, 1968).

E.M. Yamauchi, <u>Pre-Christian Gnosticism</u> (Tyndale Press, London, 1973). On Gnosticism in general, with reference to its origin, studying the main sources of evidence, not just the Nag Hammadi documents. Helpful discussion of widespread theories of Gnostic influences in the NT, based on primary texts.

W. Foerster, <u>Gnosis</u> (Clarendon Press, Oxford) is a useful collection of source material on Gnosticism; vol. 1 (1972) contains relevant patristic material; vol. 2 (1974) contains selected Nag Hammadi and Mandaean texts.

The standard bibliography is D.M. Scholer, <u>Nag Hammadi Bibliography 1948-1969</u> (E.J. Brill, Leiden, 1971). Annual supplement in <u>Novum Testamentum</u> since 1971.

THE GOSPEL OF THOMAS is probably the Gnostic document of most direct importance to NT studies. The standard Coptic text, with ET, is The Gospel According to Thomas, ed. A. Guillaumont, H.-C. Puech, et al. (E.J. Brill, Leiden and Collins, London, 1959). For English translation see also Aland's Synopsis (sec. 6 above). Note esp. the following studies:

B. Gärtner, The Theology of the Gospel of Thomas (Collins, London, 1961).
R. McL. Wilson, Studies in the Gospel of Thomas (Mowbrays, London, 1960).
W. Schrage, Das Verhältnis des Thomas-Evangeliums zur synoptischen Tradition (Töpelmann, Berlin, 1964).

(3) Patristic Literature

The standard reference works (with good biblio-graphical references to texts, translations, and secondary literature) are:

J. Quasten, Patrology (Spectrum, Utrecht/Brussels, 1950) 3 vols.
B. Altaner, Patrology (ET, Herder/Nelson, Freiburg/London-Edinburgh, 1960).

The first volume of Quasten, covering the earliest post-NT literature, is now a little dated.

The full Greek and Latin texts are to be found in the massive series, J.-P. Migne (ed.), Patrologiae Cursus Completus (Paris, 1844 ff; repr. Adler, Chicago, 1965-1971) 390 vols. All Greek and Latin Patristic texts, however obscure, included. NB also A. Hamman (ed.), Patrologiae Latinae Supplementum, 4 vols.

The recently begun series Oxford Early Christian Texts (Clarendon Press, Oxford, 1970-   ) gives original text (Greek and Latin) with ET.

For the Greek Fathers, see also the series Griechischen christlichen Schriftsteller der ersten

drei Jahrhunderte (Hinrichs, Leipzig, from c 1895;
more recent vols. from Akademie-Verlag, Berlin)
(Abbrev. GCS) A less bulky text of the Greek Fathers
is Bibliothēkē Hellēnōn Paterōn (Apostolicē Diakonia,
Athens, 1955) 57 vols. so far.

For the best texts of each individual work
consult the very comprehensive bibliographies: E.
Dekkers and A. Gaar, Clavis Patrum Latinorum [2]
(Beyaert, Bruges & Nijhoff, Hague, 1961); M. Geerard,
Clavis Patrum Graecorum (Brepols, Turnhout) - vol. 2
(1974) covers the 4th century, vol. 3 (1979) the 5th
-8th centuries. Vol. 1 is not yet published.
Invaluable, and easy to use.

A handy source for the Greek text of the early
Apologists is E.J. Goodspeed (ed.), Die Ältesten
Apologeten (Göttingen, 1914).

The Syriac Fathers have not much relevance for
NT studies. The basic source is I. Ortiz de Urbina
(ed.), Patrologia Syriaca [2] (Rome, 1965). See
further the references in Altaner's Patrology, pp.
399 ff.

The following concordances are useful for
tracing the use of NT and other vocabulary: For the
Apostolic Fathers, E.J. Goodspeed, Index Patristicus
(1907; rev. ed. Allenson, Naperville, Ill., 1960);
H. Kraft, Clavis Patrum Apostolicorum
(Wissenschaftliche Buchgesellschaft, Darmstadt,
1963). For the Apologists, E.J. Goodspeed, Index
Apologeticus (Hinrichs, Leipzig, 1912).

An invaluable tool for tracing patristic
citations of given biblical texts is Biblia
Patristica: Index des Citations et Allusions
Bibliques dans la Littérature Patristique (Centre
National de la Recherche Scientifique, Paris). Vol.
1 (1975) goes up to Clem. Alex. and Tertullian, vol.
2 (1977) up to 300, excluding Origen. Publication
continues.

The standard lexicon is G.W.H. Lampe (ed.) A
Patristic Greek Lexicon (Clarendon Press, Oxford,

1961-1968). Bauer-Arndt-Gingrich (see sec. 8)
includes references to early Christian literature.

26. GREECE AND ROME

1. Reference Works

The most convenient reference work is The
Oxford Classical Dictionary[2], ed. N.G.L. Hammond &
H.H. Scullard (Oxford UP, 1970). Good
bibliographies, though not very full.

The reference work is still 'Pauly-Wissowa',
i.e. Paulys Real-Encyclopädie der classischen
Altertumswissenschaft, ed. G. Wissowa (Stuttgart,
1894 ff) 80 large vols., and supplements still being
published! For more convenient reference, see Der
kleine Pauly: Lexicon der Antike, ed. K. Ziegler &
W. Sontheimer (Stuttgart, 1964-75), 5 vols.

2. History

The basic work is The Cambridge Ancient History,
ed. S.A. Cook, J.B. Bury, F.E. Adcock, et al
(Cambridge UP) 12 vols., covering the period from
prehistory to AD 324. The relevant volumes were
published in the 1930s, and have been only slightly
revised, if at all. An entirely new edition of
vols. I and II (in 4 vols.) has appeared (1970-75),
and a new edition of vol. III is in preparation, but
there is no prospect of an early revision of volumes
relating to the NT period. The value of the
different sections varies, depending on their
authorship. Well laid out and indexed, with good
(but old) bibliographies. Being dated, and in some
parts not above reproach, it needs checking against
more recent and more specialised works.

W.W. Tarn, Hellenistic Civilization[3], ed. G.T.
Griffith (E. Arnold, London, 1952) is extraordinarily
comprehensive for general reference.

For Roman history (and all other aspects of

Roman life and literature) a very comprehensive
reference work is being published under the title,
Aufstieg und Niedergang der römischen Welt, ed. H.
Temporini (de Gruyter, Berlin, 1972-   ). There
will be over 600 contributors, in English, French,
German and Italian; the published list of contents
suggests about 25 vols., of which more than half,
mostly very large, have appeared.

A recent large-scale work on The Emperor in the
Roman World (31 BC-AD 337) by F. Millar (Duckworth,
London, 1977) is a mine of useful information.

3. Literature

For Greek and Latin literature, use the above
reference works, and for further help find a
friendly classicist! It is too complex an area for
the non-classicist to find his way alone for more
than the cursory reference. The classical texts
most used by non-classicists are those in the Loeb
series (Greek and Latin), which give text and
English translations on opposite pages. (Published
by Heinemann, London.) All classical authors of
any importance (and quite a few others!) are in the
Loeb series.

4. Religion

A convenient introduction for the non-
specialist is H.J. Rose, Religion in Greece and Rome
(Harper & Row, New York, 1959). More wideranging is
J. Ferguson, The Religions of the Roman Empire
(Thames & Hudson, London, 1970).

The standard work on classical Greek religion
is L.R. Farnell, The Cults of the Greek States
(Clarendon Press, Oxford, 1896-1909) 5 vols. For
the Romans, a good starting-point is R.M. Ogilvie,
The Romans and their Gods in the Age of Augustus
(Chatto & Windus, London, 1969).

Relevant texts from classical authors are

usefully collected in F.C. Grant (ed.), <u>Hellenistic Religions</u> (1953) and <u>Ancient Roman Religion</u> (1957), both pub. Bobbs-Merrill, New York.

For the Mystery Religions and other oriental cults see:
G. Wagner, <u>Pauline Baptism and the Pagan Mysteries</u> (ET, Oliver & Boyd, Edinburgh, 1967). Descriptive studies and full bibliographies on the more important cults, in relation to NT thought (esp. Romans 6).
F. Cumont, <u>Astrology and Religion among the Greeks and Romans</u> (1912, repr. Dover, 1960), and <u>Oriental Religions in Roman Paganism</u>[2] (1911, repr. Dover, 1956).
R.E. Witt, <u>Isis in the Graeco-Roman World</u> (Thames & Hudson, London, 1971).
M.J. Vermaseren, <u>Mithras, the Secret God</u> (Chatto & Windus, London, 1963).

For the Hermetic Literature, the most convenient introduction for the NT student is C.H. Dodd, <u>The Interpretation of the Fourth Gospel</u> (Cambridge UP, 1953) pp. 10-53, with references to the main texts.

27. <u>MODERN LANGUAGES</u>

Most important scholarly literature is written in English, German and French. A working knowledge of <u>German</u> is essential for all scholarly research in the field of NT studies; only a small fraction of the many German monographs, articles and commentaries are ever translated into English. The proportion in <u>French</u> is much less, but much of it is very important, esp. for the Catholic viewpoint. Time spent brushing up a basic knowledge of the language from school days will be well spent.

Of course, not everyone bows to the dominance of scholarship by English, German and French. Any knowledge of Latin, Italian, Spanish, Swedish, Dutch, modern Hebrew, etc. should be jealously preserved! But for the few really essential articles or sections of commentaries in these languages, it will probably be possible to find someone to translate for you.

Learning German (and French, *mutatis mutandis*)

It is better to get a good knowledge of the basic grammar and vocabulary before tackling theological writings. One should read as much 'basic German' as possible. Paperbacks with German stories and English translation on the opposite page are useful. At a later stage, it may assist fluency to compare a good ET of a German theological book with the original. Reading of a German NT is helpful.

BBC (radio and TV) courses are excellent: books and records supplement the lessons. Language labs. are now available in many university centres. But the best method is to attend a language course in a German-speaking country, and immerse oneself in the language for a concentrated period, the longer the better. The Goethe-Institut courses are well known (Goethe-Institut, 8 München 2, Lenbachplatz 3, West Germany), but there are others which would prove equally satisfactory. (In order to benefit most fully from such a course the student should attempt to gain as full a knowledge as possible of basic grammar by himself before the course begins; this will then enable him to enter one of the higher levels at the course, rather than spending the precious time relearning the basics.) But even a language-course of a month or two will not produce instant fluency. So a chance to study in the theological faculty of a German university, preferably for a year, should be grasped without hesitation; many universities can arrange such visits, and the student should enquire about such possibilities as early as possible in the research period.

Failing the above, probably the best published 'teach-yourself' course is German for You, by D. Schulz & H. Griesbach, a graded series of paperbacks published by Longmans/Hueber. A basic introduction to German specifically for students of theology is J.D. Manton, Introduction to Theological German (Tyndale Press, London, 1971).